# TENACITY + PASSION + PATIENCE + SELF REJECTION TO FAILURE

ANTONIO E. MORALES-PITA, PhD

**RoseDog Books**
PITTSBURGH, PENNSYLVANIA 15238

RoseDog Books
585 Alpha Drive
Suite 103
Pittsburgh, PA 15238
Visit our website at *www.rosedogbookstore.com*

ISBN: 979-8-88925-041-8
eISBN: 979-8-88925-541-3

# TENACITY + PASSION + PATIENCE + SELF REJECTION TO FAILURE

# Table of Contents

# Introduction

**"If you fell down yesterday, stand up today."-**
H.G. Wells

**"There is no elevator to success. You have to take the stairs."**
Albert Einstein

**"The Greatest Glory in Living Lies Not in Never Falling, But in Rising Every Time We fall"**
Nelson Mandela

Importance of tenacity and standing up after a physical or intellectual fall.

The word tenacity, as defined in Google, is the quality or fact of being able to: a) grip something firmly; b) very determined, determined, or c) continuing to exist.

In this author's forthcoming book *Grit+Tenacity+ Proactiveness (Pulling the Bull by the Horns)*, to be published by Austin Macauley Publisher in 2022, he wrote that tenacity is a gift or attitude to reach goals.

Citing his own words: "Since I was young man —and in the natural process of getting older— whenever I hear news about somebody achieving outstanding results, tenacity is always mentioned as an important reason for the success. Tenacity is indispensable for training the brain, and the body, for fostering the will to succeed. Whenever we talk about a scientific discovery, an athlete breaking records, an outstanding artist or singer who has been able to stand out as a singer, an actor, a composer, an orchestra leader, or a musical director the word 'tenacity' is reiteratively mentioned."

Delving into the root of tenacity's importance, one can learn about the courage and the iron will needed to repeat an experiment until he/she reaches a minimum level of perfection, to fall and to stand up again, to go to extremes of tiredness and to start all over again. Repetition is necessary because it is rare to achieve something extraordinary in a single try. To approve a medicine in the health industry many scientists or specialists must invest years to experimentation involving persons—or sometimes even animals —of different ages and sexes, in several seasons and countries. For a singer to reach fame, he/she must practice reiteratively, to improve his/her singing. A singer must learn to accept low paying jobs at the beginning until he/she acquires prestige, must learn to show his/her talent in different stages, theaters, countries, must learn to be healthy; and, finally, must learn to meet all the requirements stated under different circumstances.

Deeply meditating on the common factors in all successful individuals, one can see the following: (1). A successful individual must have the talent of tenacity to reach the goal. (2). He/she must be completely committed to the objective he/she is pursuing. (3). The systematic repetition of attempts is indispensable while working towards the goal. (4). These exercises are conceived to be long range, not short or intermediate. (5). There must exist the conviction — or the very strong ineluctable desire and need — to reach the goal.

## The role of tenacity in standing up after a physical or intellectual fall

Human beings usually wish, dream about, work hard to achieve goals. They may need time, patience, and tenacity to go on after receiving a rejection of a project, a dream, an ambition, or even a spiritual or material aspiration.

There are two choices; a) to give up the goal as if they were impossible to conquer; or b) to insist looking for alternative approaches, to deeply analyze the need or the feasibility of achieving the objective or target; to decide to go ahead through the thick and thin.

During my life as a scholar, I faced two huge occasions, in which my iron will was threatened by reality, and I fell and couldn't achieve my goal; but my tenacity stood up and after a while it imposed itself: 1. My self-assigned goal to attain my second PhD in Ukraine in 1990; 2. To recover my passport—retained by the Cuban Communist Party of the University of Havana— for 6 months and leave Cuba for good.

<u>My self-assigned goal to attain my second PhD in Ukraine in 1990</u>. In Cuba there were in 1990 only two scholars holding 2 PhD in economics. After returning to Cuba with my first PhD, I created a research team, with two faculty and students in their last year. I traveled twice to the Soviet Union to write and to conclude my second dissertation. I had to write and pub-

lish three books as part of my last dissertation and to present a document signed by the Ministry of Sugar stating that my research was useful for the Cuban economy, and to travel to the former Soviet Union for the third time. It took me eight years experiencing "n" with falls and "n+1" subsequent stands up.

The relations between the governments of Cuba and the Soviet Union were tense. The Soviets did not want to cover the cost of my last six-month stay in Kiev, Ukraine, and Cuba (for the first time) had to take care of my basic expenditures in rubles. At the end of the fifth month, I delivered the final version of the dissertation, and it was returned to me full of corrections to be done in three weeks. I felt unable to redo the dissertation. This was a very painful fall. When I got back to my room, I was very sad.

Next morning, I woke up full of energy and decided that I had to finish it in three weeks. I could not return to Cuba without finishing my dissertation. I had to type around three hundred pages in a Russian typewriter; fortunately, I received help from the person in charge of the library, and finally I could successfully defend my last dissertation.

Given the tense situation between Cuba and the US (which finally disappeared one year later) I thought I would never receive the diploma in Russian. I had picked up letters from each member of the committee stating their decision to grant the 2nd PhD, which was corroborated by the Cuban National Scientific Committee.

I had the peace of mind of having done all I could to finish my second doctorate; but, without that document, my second doctorate would not be accepted internationally. Three years later, the diploma was found in one desk at the office of the

Cuban Ministry of Higher Education in Moscow, miraculously was recovered and sent to Havana.

I never gave up, and I had the diploma in my hands three years after my defense. Without tenacity I wouldn't have been able to finish the hardest scientific achievement of my life.

<u>To recover my passport – retained by the Cuban Ministry of Higher Education- during my last stay in Cuba in 1995-1996</u>

On July 17, 1995, I returned to Havana for one week because I had received a fax, letting me know that my mother was very seriously ill. I needed to see her for the last time. As I had been doing since 1993, I went to the international affairs department of the University of Havana to drop off my passport for its regular upgrading and went on my way to distribute the Mexican gifts to my family and friends.

As my stay in Havana was supposed to last one week, I only took $100 U.S with me and a minimum amount of clothing. My luggage was now empty after I had dropped off all the gifts I brought to my folks. Despite the public transportation difficulties of the city of Havana, my first visit to my mother was encouraging. She had had a stroke. She was taking some pills that I sent her from Mexico, and her memory and uncontrolled behavior were improving. I promised to see her at least twice before returning to Mexico. My children were all right. I loved them and felt happy to see them and pamper their desire to dress in Mexican clothes.

The process of upgrading the passport normally took two days. My airline ticket back to Mexico was dated July 24. On the morning of July 21, I went to the international affairs department to pick up my upgraded passport. To my surprise, the passport was not ready. I was informed that the Minister of

Higher Education had recently issued a regulation banning Cuban professors from staying abroad more than two years in a row. I had already exceeded that limit in three months. An order had come directly from the President of the University of Havana not to upgrade my passport.

For me it is difficult to find an English word to describe how I felt. I was simply stunned. The feeling was like walking on apparently solid ground; and suddenly feeling the ground crack and shake under one's feet, and then being on the brink of a chasm. I had left Mexico in an organized way, and my work was ready to be resumed as soon as I had returned. A state-wide event about environment was to be held with the participation of several institutions, and I was the president of that event. Twenty-five graduate students were working with me on their theses, and three of them were about to finish their work. I had already scheduled classes at three universities. Oh, my goodness! My life was so beautiful in Mexico! I felt alive, and useful! During my two-year stay in Mexico, I had implemented the knowledge acquired during thirty years of research work in Cuba, Scotland, and Ukraine. My life seemingly had greater worth in Mexico. In Cuba I had little to do. Practically nobody there really wanted to work. Most instructors at the College of Economics were only waiting for the opportunity to go abroad to live like human beings. On top of the precarious economic situation of the country, the people were generally discouraged about the system. It was a hopeless life. My mind just could not come to grips with the situation. Would I have to accept that arbitrary action taken by the Minister of Higher Education in open violation of international agreements? My work in Mexico was supported by a contract with the Mexican governmental agency for scientific research. How could the Cuban authorities be so disrespectful? How could they condemn a man who had given the best years of his life to his country, who was now reaching his full potential abroad, to stay in Cuba without doing anything useful?

The situation was even more incomprehensible because my work in Mexico was responsible for my sending about one thousand dollars per month to the ministry of Higher Education in Cuba. My staying and working in Havana would not provide them with a single dollar.

My thoughts were going in circles. I could not understand the order banning my return to Mexico. I then couldn't see any way out and fell. But I didn't give up. I just had to find the way to stand up.

An idea came to my mind. I have always fought for what I thought to be right. I had never given in without fighting for my rights. I decided I had to do something to enable me to return to Mexico. Up to that moment, I had an acceptable relationship with the Minister of Higher Education. He had helped me to return to Kiev when the Soviet Union did not have money to pay my living expenses. It was he who had placed two medals on my chest for outstanding scientific work in 1983 and 1985. I had met with him after my return from receiving my last doctorate, and he had congratulated me for being the first economist in the University of Havana to get a second doctorate. In 1991, he had signed an agreement with the Minister of Sugar so that my scientific methods could be applied, at last, to the 1991 sugar crop. I thought he appreciated me and that perhaps he could make an exception to the rule he had just created.

Unfortunately, although the Minister accepted to interview me, his answer was no. The result of the meeting with the Minister was the second blow of that same day, but this was stronger than the first one. After the first impact, I had hoped to persuade the Minister. After the second disappointing blow, I was convinced that I could not return to Mexico in July and that I had to wait Heaven knew for how long. The first set back had been a surprise, shook my optimism, and depressed me. The second set back was not unexpected; it made me more aware of the reality I was about to live, but surprisingly did not depress me. I had absolutely decided to fight for my freedom. I did not know how or when, I would leave Cuba, but I decided to do so for good as soon as feasible.

In my book *Havana-Merida-Chicago (A Journey to Freedom) 2nd version* – which is now in the process of being published in 2023 – the readers would be able to see how I could finally recover my passport by standing up on several occasions as well as the original way in which my wife and I communicated using a very special mail system.

At the end of the day, I could stand up, this time with my wife's help, and the Mexican institution's where I was working with for three years.

## Food for thought

1. Have any of the readers found themselves in similar situations as narrated by the author in this chapter?
2. If they fell, were they able to stand up, and keep on their lives?
3. Have any of them succeeded in achieving a goal without any previous failure?

# CHAPTER I
## The Role of Passion in the Battle between Tenacity and Procrastination

**"Never put off till tomorrow what may be done day after tomorrow just as well."**
Mark Twain

**"Only put off until tomorrow what you are willing to die having left undone"**
Pablo Picasso

**"I never put off till tomorrow what I can possibly do - the day after."**
Oscar Wilde

**"You cannot escape the responsibility of tomorrow by evading it today."**
Abraham Lincoln

**The opposing extremes between passion and procrastination**

Browsing through different sources the definitions of passion, and procrastination the author selected the following:

According to Google, passion is defined as a) a strong and barely controllable emotion, or an outburst of strong emotion. An intense desire or enthusiasm for something; b) according to Webster's New World Dictionary of the American Language Second College Edition 1986 by Simon and Schuster, passion usually implies a strong emotion that has an overpowering or compelling effect.

According to Webster's the verb to procrastinate is to put off doing something unpleasant or burdensome until a future time, or to postpone (such actions) indefinitely. According to Oxford American Dictionary to procrastinate is to postpone an action, to be dilatory. The author of this book has not found the verb "to procrastinate" in Spanish, rather through synonyms like to postpone indefinitely, to be dilatory, not to a single verb.

While I was teaching in Cuban and Mexican universities, I had not heard about the word procrastination, but I felt its negative impact on my students. In other words, I was aware of the damage that procrastination had done like poor grades (because the students had postponed studying until the days previous to the exams) systematic late or incomplete attendance, along with interstudy consulting among students shortly before the beginning of the exams. I could feel the nervousness and fear of the procrastinating students especially before the exams. Another way to procrastinate was to ask the professor in a "subtle" way if a given difficult topic was subject to appear in the exams. Very few of all my ten thousand students around the world were "A" students (usually between ten to fifteen% of the whole group).

The damage created by procrastination went beyond the classroom and is also present in the professionals who experience lacks knowledge that should have been acquired in their studies hadn't they procrastinated and dedicated more time to deeply study the different subject matters.

In other words, to study not with the primary purpose of learning, rather by trying to guess what topic should appear in the exams. These types of students may not be not aware of the fact that the professor can explain part of the content of everyday class. If, on top of that, they try to guess what could appear as a question in an exam, they are reducing their possibilities of learning how to face the problems and difficulties they will experience after graduating and starting to work as college specialist. As a matter of fact, the professors — of economics and especially international political economy at least — cannot teach about specific issues their students will face when they start working.

Life is constantly changing. Just to cite a simple example, around the first and second decades of this century, Greece was facing a terrible economic and financial situation in the change from the drachma to the euro. When I visited Greece as a tourist in 2022, I expected to be beggars all over the place, sadness, strikes, and so on. What did I find? Well, Greece had considerably overcome its financial issues. Its GDP growth went from 3.4% in January 2021 to 2.3% in January 2022, according to the National Statistical Service of Greece. I visited five cities from north to south and could feel good mood everywhere I went. In all the cities where I stayed, restaurants were packed all the time, while the countryside showed fertile land, no uncultivated areas.

How had I detected the effects of procrastination in the academic field? This author has met some faculty members who are afraid of writing and delivering papers for publication assuming that they would be criticized by colleagues. I met very intelligent scholars who wrote thesis or dissertations and never defended them, demanding from themselves always something better that would be wholeheartedly accepted by the scholarly opponents.

I was able to defeat procrastination because I was never afraid of being criticized. When I wrote my master's thesis, as soon as I finished it, I delivered the paper to my advisor. I felt sure that I had done a valuable contribution which was not exempt from mistakes. By the way, I learned from my critics about ways to improve my papers. I wrote two dissertations in Russian and met opposition from colleagues who were afraid of being criticized.

My first "scholarly" paper was based on my master's thesis. In the first number of the journal Economia y Desarrollo, created by the college of Economics of the University of Havana in 1972, there were three papers: two taken from abroad, and one written by this Cuban.

I never believed to be "perfect". I tried hard to do things well. For example, while teaching, whenever I made a mistake, I recognized it publicly so as not to confuse my students.

In order to defeat procrastination one has to believe in oneself, ready to accept criticism. Whenever I had to undertake a task, or to face a challenge, I always said to myself: "Antonio, you never say 'no' to yourself. Let others deny whatever you want to face." Do whatever you can to fulfill your purposes in life.

In my book Havana-Merida-Chicago. *A Journey to Freedom*, the readers can find plenty of obstacles I had to face to hold both my first and my second PhD. I always believed in myself, and was decided to do whatever I was asked, in order to achieve my goals. I might have been temporarily defeated; but, almost immediately, I could stand up and try new avenues.

As a househusband after my wife died, I had to face innumerable tasks which I had never previously done. I had to cook, to be organized in always placing things in the same place, to have my house clean, especially to clean the kitchen every day, to keep busy singing, healthy, ready to undertake whatever unpredictable task appeared in front of my eyes. It wasn't easy to undertake the new tasks, but I was done to do them regardless of whatever difficulty I had to face. It felt so well when one learns something new and make it work! Attempt to congratulate yourself. Celebrate the results of exercising, trying successfully to improve as a human being.

Some years ago, I had always loved to exercise, but not every day. As time went by and grew older, regardless whether I was ready to do it every day now I say to myself: " Go ahead, young man, do it right now. Do not postpone it unless an incredible difficulty forces you to do. But, as soon as possible, do whatever you had to postpone."

I had always loved to walk although I was limited to a certain distance. As recently as in July 2022, I self-assigned the task of walking one mile per day. According to my iphone comparing average walking and running distances are the following:

a. In 2021 1.1 miles/day and in 2022 so far 1.5 miles/day.
b. Trending: last week 7,136 steps, and the last eight weeks was 3,464 steps.
c. I have increased my goal from 1 mile to two miles per day.

One of the most important outcomes of this effort is that I feel healthy, my muscles are responding so well to my extra effort. I see excellent results in sleeping at least seven hours per day. I have been using a cane for five years, but now I walk with holding the cane sometimes in the air, not on the floor. I am improving my balance.

## The confrontation between tenacity and procrastination

About the power of tenacity over procrastination, this author came across very 25 profound and convincing examples of successful sportsman and women in the bleached Report https"//The most Astounding Athletes Career Comeback.

I am partially citing only seven of the twenty-five examples: " Here they go:

- **Michael Jordan**
  Burdened with grief from the murder of his father, "His Airness," chose to retire from basketball in 1993. After a lackluster stint as a minor league ball player, Jordan made his famous two-word announcement to the world: "I'm back."

  But many suspected MJ wouldn't be all that he once was, and he wasn't, at first. That is to say his play was spectacular, but not ethereal.

  Turns out though, that after a year and a half away from the game, Jordan just needed a bit more warming up. The next three seasons would be another Bulls three-peat.

- **Jim Morris**

  Teenaged **Jim Morris** was a hot pick in the amateur baseball draft back in the early 80s. But then his pitching arm rebelled. According to the article Jim Morris - Derailed By Arm Injuries, Morris "had several operations, including one that involved replacing a tendon in his left elbow with one from his right ankle." Nothing worked. Morris gave up baseball, became a teacher and settled into middle class life in the suburbs.

  More than 10 years later, 35-year-old Morris dazzled the scouts at an open MLB tryout by throwing not 1, not 2, not 5, not 10, but 12 consecutive 98 mph pitches. In his first time on the mound as a major league pitcher, the aged rookie struck out Royce Clayton of the Texas Rangers in 4 pitches.

- **Mohammad Ali**

  Three and a half years. That's how long Muhammad Ali was suspended from boxing at the height of his professional career. The suspension was a result of his claim for conscientious objector status after the U.S. military drafted him to fight in Vietnam.

  Ali lost "The Fight of the Century" against Frazier in 1970, but later beat him in a rematch, then, in the same year, beat reigning champion George Foreman. Ali kept fighting until 1981.

- **Monica Seles**

  She was number one in the World Rankings—at that time the youngest woman ever to top the chart. Her game only got better over the next couple years.

  But in 1993, when many felt she was at her peak, a deranged man reached over a court side railing and plunged a blade in her back. Monica disappeared from the tennis scene for more than two years. When she did come back, she won the Canadian Open in August of 1995, and the Australian open in January of 1996.

- **Joe Simpson**

  He shattered his leg while making a first ascent of the west face of a remote peak in the Andes. After a failed attempt to lower him to safety, his climbing partner cut the rope to save his own life, and left Simpson to die. Simpson fell off the side of the mountain and down into a crevasse.

  Instead of succumbing to death in an icy tomb, he somehow made his way back out to the surface, and then spent three days clawing his way across a glacier, over boulders, around a lake, then finally back to camp.

  Doctors said he would never climb again, and maybe not even walk well. Yet after numerous operations and 2 years of physical therapy, he was out on the peaks again.

- **Niki Lauda**

  In 1976, on his way to a second World Championship Title in Formula One racing, Niki Lauda hit a little bump in the road; he wiped out during a race. His car burst into flames, skidded back out onto the track, and was broadsided by another car. Lauda got torched inside his Ferrari; much of his face was incinerated before he was pulled to safety. He bled internally, lapsed into a coma. It was touch and go for a few days, but Lauda pulled through.

  Forty-three days later, he was behind the wheel at the Italian Grand Prix. Lauda would go on to win two more championship titles before retiring.

- **Greg Lemond**

  Your typical story of boy wins the Tour de France, boy breaks wrist in subsequent race, boy goes turkey hunting and gets blasted full of buckshot by his brother-in-law, boy loses three-quarters of his blood in-route to the hospital, boy's chest is slit open and doctors drain the blood from around his collapsed lung, boy survives although one finger is shattered and thirty-five pellets remain in his body (including three in his heart and five in his liver), boy takes two years to recover and starts racing again despite crippling pain, boy wins the Tour de France again (and then again.)"

The seven athletes' examples reconfirm that they had to be tenacious, and to overcome procrastination in order to succeed.

They fell several times but always stood up successfully and became reiterated champions.

When in 2016 as a tourist I visited three famous eastern Canadian cities, Ottawa, Quebec, and Montreal. Montreal impressed me like a very friendly city, but also because over there I was unforgettably impressed when I saw the statue of a young man running with only one leg. When I learned that he was a national hero and an inspirational figure for his battle against cancer, I was profoundly impressed and couldn't avoid tears coming out of my eyes. This was only one year after Gladys' death, who was such an empathetic person.

From Terry Fox, Biography, Marathon of Hope, & Facts, Britannica, I transcribed the following three paragraphs:

"Born in 1958 in Winnipeg. Manitoba, Canada, he was born on July 28, 1958 and died on June 28, 1981New Westminster, British Columbia), Canadian activist who became a national hero and an inspirational figure for his battle against cancer. Through his Marathon of Hope event, a race across Canada, he raised millions of dollars for cancer research.

At age 10 Fox moved with his family to Port Coquitlam, British Columbia. In 1977, while attending Simon Fraser University, Fox was diagnosed with cancer. The disease's progression led to the amputation of one of his legs above the knee.

Fox soon learned to run using an artificial leg, and by 1979 he was able to complete a marathon (26.2 miles [42 km]). A few months later he decided to run across Canada in order to raise money for cancer research. His run, which he called the Marathon of Hope, began in St. John's, Newfoundland, on April 12, 1980. Initially Fox did not receive much attention or money, but that changed as he continued to run, covering up to 30 miles (48 km) per day. Fox passed the halfway point in eastern Ontario, but on September 1, 1980, chest pains forced him to stop just outside the city of Thunder Bay.

It was soon discovered that the cancer had spread to his lungs, and he was unable to continue. By that time Fox had covered 3,339 miles (5,374 km) and had raised some $1.7 million (Canadian). In early 1981 the Marathon of Hope surpassed Fox's goal of $24 million in donations. Despite undergoing numerous treatments, Fox died on June 28, 1981. Prior to his death, the government had made him the youngest ever Companion of the Order of Canada, and he was twice named Canadian of the Year. Terry Fox Runs, which are organized by the Terry Fox Foundation, are held annually in cities throughout Canada and other countries."

## Food for thought

1. Are some of the readers still hopeful to succeed the first time that they are pursuing any goal?
2. Through the examples cited in this chapter, do some readers feel inspired to stand up after a fall, maybe not only once, but also more than once?
3. Are some of the readers aware of the ways procrastinating efforts can oppose achieving success?

# CHAPTER II
## Is There any Relationship between Tenacity and Patience?

**"Patience and tenacity are worth more than twice their weight in cleverness."**
Unknown

**"Tenacity and patience pay off."**
Unknown

**"Persist until something happens."**
Unknown

**If an individual is tenacious, would it be easy for him/ her to be patient?**

Very famous persons have deeply analyzed the relationship between being patient and tenacious.

According to.

a. Ms. Robin Luftig, Robin is an **award-nominated columnist** for magazines such as Leading Hearts,

CBN.com, and many more Her definition for patience is *"the capacity for waiting: the ability to endure waiting, delay, or provocation without becoming annoyed or upset, or to persevere calmly when faced with difficulties."* . For Ms. Luftig, tenacious is defined as *"determined or stubborn: tending to stick firmly to any decision, plan, or opinion without changing or doubting it."*

b.  Ralph Waldo Emerson said, *"Adopt the pace of nature; her secret is patience."* Ralph Waldo Emerson (May 25, 1803 – April 27, 1882), who went by his middle name Waldo, was an American essayist, lecturer, philosopher, abolitionist, and poet who led the transcendentalist movement of the mid-19th century

c.  Joyce Meyer stated, *"Patience is not simply the ability to wait — it's how we behave while we're waiting.* Pauline Joyce Meyer is an American Charismatic Christian author, speaker, and president of Joyce Meyer Ministries.

d.  The Rev. Billy Graham once said, *"Each life is made up of mistakes and learning, waiting and growing, practicing patience and being persistent."* **William Franklin Graham Jr.** (November 7, 1918 – February 21, 2018) was an American evangelist and an ordained Southern Baptist minister who became well known internationally in the late 1940s. He was a prominent evangelical Christian figure, and according to a biographer, was "among the most influential Christian leaders" of the 20th century.[2]

e.  Mark Twain "Patience is a virtue, and I am learning patience. It's a tough lesson". "Patience is the art of hiding impatience." Samuel Langhorne Clemens (November 30, 1835 – April 21, 1910), known by his pen name Mark Twain, was **an American writer, humorist, entrepreneur, publisher, and lecturer.** He was lauded as the "greatest humorist the United States has produced",

   f. John Quincy Adams "Patience and perseverance have a magical effect before which difficulties disappear and obstacles vanish". "Try and fail, but don't fail to try" John Quincy Adams was an American statesman, diplomat, lawyer, and diarist who served as the sixth president of the United States, from 1825 to 1829.

In itself, the fact that so many famous Americans have approached and developed the concepts of tenacity and patience justify that this author includes them into this chapter.

## This author's experience handling the duo "tenacity and patience"

What is my experience simultaneously handling patience and tenacity? First of all, I am an inborn tenacious man. Whenever I face an obstacle in my personal and scientific careers, automatically I feel motivated to face it; and as soon as possible, to overcome it. Only under especial circumstances, the shadow of procrastination dares to appear in my life. What about patience? Well, this doesn't come at the same speed as tenacity. As a matter of fact, on some occasions while I was in my twenties, thirties, forties, and even fifties, I had to force myself to be patient. It is not an automatic behavior because sometimes my tenacity pushes me to act, especially in relation to my feelings. I have made several mistakes because I haven't waited some days before making an important decision.

Since I was born in 1940, my tenacity hasn't slowed down by turning eighty; but my patience is holding me much more to undertake an action than I was young. Which are the main reasons that justify my being patient? Some of the precipitated actions taken by me – whenever I faced a setback or a predicament in relation to unforeseen important obstacles – had not always been successful.

Example. 1- To interrupt my secondary education, accepting my mother's request to study English when I was fourteen years old to help my family's economic situation. I didn't want to interrupt my eighth grade, but I was forced anyway. It was my mother's decision, not mine. A second most important decision I had to make when I was placed at a level of sixth grade with a minimal knowledge of English. My mother was not patient, and I had to accept her decision. I had to make an extraordinary effort. Therefore, I was tenacious in accepting a hard task, but there was no time for waiting.

Example 2 – When I was doing the third year of high school, my boss at the office I was working offered me the opportunity of learning economics as a subject, and I accepted it but I wasn't told that it would be to start a bachelor's degree in economics. Since I hadn't finished high school, I declined the proposal, but I was forced to enter the university of Havana. So, in reality, it was not my decision, but I had the unwanted responsibility of studying a bachelor's degree without finishing High School. I didn't have time to think it over, I was forced to accept the change in studies.

Example 3 – Before finishing my bachelor's degree, I was chosen to become a "professor" to my peers. This time, I made the decision without the possibility of being patient again.

Example 4 – After teaching for two years as young professor of Operational Research, I was given the option of studying a master's degree in Great Britain. I had one week to think about it. Therefore, I had the option of waiting or rejecting the proposal, but I decided to accept the challenge.

Example 5 – While studying my master's degree, I learned of the PhD. My opportunity was to do it in Havana, without any mentor, but I had acquired research experience while doing my bachelor's degree. I followed the established procedure for doing the PhD in Havana, starting with a dissertation. My colleagues rejected my pre-defense, and I had to wait almost a year to conclude my second dissertation; since I was helped by a Soviet scientist dwelling temporarily in Havana, after waiting patiently for four years, I could go to Kiev, through overcoming four pre-defenses, and became PhD.

Example 6 – My decision to ask for asylum in the United States Consulate in Merida.

After returning to Mexico, my wife and I originally tried to ask for asylum in Merida, but – despite my wife's connections within the Mexican government – it was never received. We had spent more than three months in Mexico and were receiving calls from the University of Havana.

Now comes a genuine confrontation between tenacity and patience. We were totally done not to return to Cuba, had not received asylum from Mexico; and consequently, our decision was crystal clear. Since Gladys did not know English at all, I asked her if she were ready to go with me to the US. Her answer was "Yes".

There was no need whatsoever to wait for an action, namely, to knock on the door of the American Consul in Merida, with a copy of my curriculum vitae, and in less than a week, we received our visas to visit the United States.

In conclusion, out of the six occasions in the duo "wait" and "not to wait", numbers 1,2, and 3 I was forced "not to wait", numbers 4 and 6 I decided "not to wait" and finally number 5 circumstances absolutely beyond my control forced me to wait.

## Is it possible to be simultaneously tenacious and impatient?

Yes, this is quite likely. The more tenacious happens to be a human being, the harder it is for him/her to be patient. There is an old saying that I remember from my childhood, coming specifically from my parents, "It is easier to stop a tenacious person in a hurry than to encourage a slower person to go faster". My parents, especially my mother, was always busy. For example, if I needed a button of my shirt to be sewed, it was faster for her to sew by button, than for me than to take off my shirt.

My father didn't allow her to work outside home although she was always busy with several self-assigned tasks. After my father retired from his forty years as stevedore in the Havana central market, he allowed her to work as a seamstress in a small factory some blocks away from home. Well, after two months working in the factory, my mother broke all records in different types of job, she won a prize and became famous for her productivity. At the time she already was seventy years old.

Everybody knew that if he/she needed some work to be done quickly, my mother was the person to be asked.

While at the University of Havana, I was studying or even teaching, I was so busy that I did not have time for friends, except for girlfriends. I was used to be in a hurry. When it came to the time of undertaking a master's degree abroad, I immediately enrolled in a foreign language course without thinking it twice. I loved to learn whatever subject matter I had internally or externally been assigned to. In other words, at least until turning thirty, I was never fundamentally patient.

My colleagues at the University of Havana, and also in other universities abroad were different. Some of them thought it twice before starting a research project, or even teaching new courses, and of course a graduate course They were naturally patient. I was not.

I became a close friend to one of my colleagues. We both were able to write dissertations, but I was riskier than he. I knew I could make mistakes, but I wasn't afraid to be criticized. Despite he wrote one-of-a-kind dissertation, he never became PhD because he was never happy with his work, and always was trying to improve it on his own. Unfortunately, he died in his fifties without defending his dissertation. He was too patient. I wasn't.

When I was a student, I always sat in the first row to be closer to my teachers. I was never afraid to ask. On one occasion, I asked a question to my advisor in his classroom, and he laughed at me in public. I didn't care, insisted on my ignorance, and requested his help. As a matter of fact, he had made a slight mistake, which he did not want to recognize. He stood in front of the board staring at the location of my question. His answer to me, addressing the whole classroom, was: "I am happy to see that somebody was paying due attention to the blackboard, because on purpose I had introduced a mistake. Yes, there should be another word instead of whatever."

Since I had been teaching in one university in Cuba, in several universities in Mexico, and in three universities in the US, I had taught approximately 10,000 students, I have never hesitated to recognize a mistake I had made in class. I have generally been tenacious and impatient. Of course, I have met professors who have been tenacious and patient, like my unforgettable teacher of mathematics in High School. I am taking one paragraph on page 30 of my book *Is It Possible to Inspire Anyone?*

"<u>Aníbal Roger</u>, my mathematics teacher in high school, showed me what a good educator was about. He was patient; he cared about his students. His pedagogical objective was to be understood, not to show off his knowledge, and he wanted to get his message across to everyone in the class – from the best student to the one who was struggling to pass. He showed me the importance of applying knowledge acquired in the classroom to real life. Although he passed away some years ago, he remains my inspiration as an educator. His patience and self-control are unforgettable."

## Another example of being tenacious and impatient, this time in my relationship with my wife trying to stop smoking

During the first years of arriving with Gladys to this country I participated in an intense working activity. On various occasions we had arguments occasioned by lack of time together. She was not a heavy smoker, but she had acquired the vice of smoking. I had never smoked in my life. Smelling smoke in my clothes made me feel uncomfortable. I was aware of the damage that smoking does on our lungs. I did not find out why she started to smoke at an early age and was not able to be in her shoes. Sometimes, while accompanying her to the doctor's office, I witnessed how intensely he insisted on her to stop smoking after having seen some X-ray plates showing advancement of her pulmonary sickness.

It would have been all right to try to persuade her to stop smoking, but not to the point of being rude with her demanding that she stops smoking in a brief period. We argued to the point of insulting her, and even threating her with a divorce. She started to cry reciprocating my insults with complaints of lack of understanding how hard it was for her to stop smoking.

After a while of the argument, I sat down to pray alone. Yes, I should have been more patient with her. She loved me unconditionally and had given me a large number of genuine proofs of her exceptionally unique form of loving me during decades.

I was rude, blunt, and bruising with my wife demanding that she stop smoking in a brief period. I wasn't fair, and couldn't hold my tears... I felt to have been unjustly cruel with her. After a while I asked her forgiveness of my selfish and "machista" unfair attitude. Folding her hands with mine, I promised to the Lord not to do it again. After that, I never did it again.

She was able to forgive me.

In this example my impatience hurt my wife and me.

Meditating and learning from this experience helped me to be supporting, understanding, and loving when Gladys had to suffer the dire consequences of not having stopped smoking on her lungs in previous decades.

In my book *Gladys, My Unforgettable Love* I narrated the moment in which she stopped smoking, which unfortunately happened when her pulmonary sickness had become irremediable. The same day in which her physician showed Gladys the X-ray indicated threatening shadows in the lungs, and he demanded her to stop the addiction right then.

"That same day, she sat down alone in the living room, staring at box of cigarettes with which she started a monologue. She needed to be alone. She did not want to hide the box of cigarettes and pretend that she had overcome the addition. During some days she had been doing so, and finally she stopped smoking"

My answer to the question Is it possible to be simultaneously tenacious and impatient? is Yes.


**Food for thought**

1.  Have reading this chapter reminded the readers of their own experiences of patiently waiting or impatiently not waiting occasions?
2.  Did they feel more prepared to force themselves to wait before facing a dilemma?
3.  What about standing up after a fall? Do they feel prepared to overcome procrastination if it happens to be present in this waiting or not waiting experience

# CHAPTER III

## Does procrastination play any role in the interaction between tenacity and patience?

Famous phrases about procrastination

**"Procrastination is something best put off until tomorrow"**
Gerald Vaughan

**"Continuous improvement is better than delayed perfection"**
Mark Twain

**"Procrastination is the grave in which opportunity is buried"**
@ derandomizes

**"Procrastination is opportunity's assassin"**
Victor Kian

**"Procrastination is the thief of time"**
Charles Dicken

**"Action will destroy your Procrastination"**
Og Mandi no

Analyzing the six phrases, procrastination is associated with inaction; therefore, it can be considered to be somewhat indirectly related to patience. By the same token, patience doesn't imply inaction. It is always sensible to meditate for a short period of time about what type of action is more relevant to the being faced situation.

While patience doesn't necessarily mean to stop the process of deciding, then procrastination doesn't have to mediate between patience and tenacity.

The more complex is the decision to be made, then patience will allow extra time to make up one's mind, and to behave in a tenacious way.

## Does defeating procrastination open the door to improving tenacity?

According to Wikipedia, "…procrastination is the action of unnecessarily and voluntarily delaying or postponing something despite knowing that there will be negative consequences for doing so. From cultural and social perspectives, students from both Western and non-Western cultures are found to exhibit academic procrastination, but for different reasons. Students from Western cultures tend to procrastinate in order to avoid doing worse than they have done before or from failing to learn as much as they should have, whereas students from non-Western cultures tend to procrastinate in order to avoid looking incompetent, or to avoid demonstrating a lack of ability in front of their peers. It is also important to consider how different cultural perspectives of time management can impact procrastination. For example, in cultures that have a multi-active view of time, people tend to place a higher value on making sure a job is done accurately before finishing. In cultures with a linear view of time, people tend to designate a certain amount of time on a task and stop once the allotted time has expired."

Browsing through Google about ways to defeat procrastination, this author found an interesting paper by Ms. Kendra Cherry entitled Tips for Overcoming Procrastination Updated on July 19, 2020.

## Top Tips for Overcoming Procrastination (verywellmind.com)

The paper recommends seven steps which, in my opinion, can help procrastinators if they really wish to feel more useful to themselves by overcoming this undesirable disorder.

## Tip # 1 — Deal with Your Fear.

"Fear is one factor that contributes to procrastination. This can involve a fear of failure, a fear of making mistakes, or even a fear of success. "

## Tip # 2 — Make a List

"Start by creating a to-do list with things that you would like to accomplish. If necessary, put a date next to each item if there is a deadline that you need to meet."

## Tip # 3 — Projects Down into More Manageable Segments

"When you are faced with a big project, you might feel daunted, intimidated, or even hopeless when you look at the sheer amount of work involved. At this point, take individual items on your list and break them down into a series of steps."

### Tip # 4 — Recognize the Onset of Procrastination

" As you start to tackle items on your list, pay attention to when thoughts of procrastination start to creep into your mind. If you find yourself thinking "I don't feel like doing this now" or "I'll have time to work on this later," then you need to recognize that you are about to procrastinate."

### Tip # 5 — Eliminate Distractions

"It's hard to get any real work done when you keep turning your attention to what's on television or you keep checking your friends' Facebook status updates."

### Tip # 6 — Reward Yourself

"Once you have completed a task (or even a small portion of a larger task), it is important to reward yourself for your efforts."

### Tip # 7 — Final Thoughts

"Breaking the procrastination habit isn't easy. After all, if it was simple there wouldn't be an estimated 80% to 95% of students engaging in procrastination on a regular basis. The urge to put things off can be strong, especially when there are so many things around us to provide fun and entertaining distractions."

This author is completely in agreement with the seven steps recommended by Ms. Cherry. Generally speaking, I have rarely detected the presence of procrastination in my life, because I am an inborn tenacious individual. Going through the seven steps:

- **Tip #1.** Fear. Whenever I face a new task, most of the time I think positively and emphasize the importance of accomplishing it. For example, when I was chosen for starting a master's degree, first of all I took it as a recognition for my excellent results in the Bachelor of Economics degree. I had the second highest average of 94.2 among 100 senior students. Secondly, I knew I could speak, write, and read English because of my legitimate vocation for my second language. I started to work as a bilingual stenographer when I was sixteen years old and had spent 29 days speaking English all the time during my first travel abroad. My being the student with the third largest average among thirty British students also corroborated my believe on my own possibilities. Thirdly, when I was in Britain, I learned of the PhD, and fought very hard to be the first professor at the College of Economics at the University of Havana because of my previous experience in doing research on my own.

- **Tip #2.** Making a List. Since I have always been very busy, starting my teaching career, doing research, writing papers, and books, studying foreign languages like Italian and French, almost daily I was used to make a list of the different activities. At the end of each day, I self-checked my results. If any of the tasks was not finished, I would immediately include it in the following day.

- **Tip #3.** Introducing of Managing Segments. Projects Down into More Manageable Segments. Given the fact that I was normally busy studying, teaching, preparing classes, I had to break down the tasks into easily approachable sub-tasks. Most of the time I had planned tasks in order of urgency and difficulty.

- **Tip #4.** Defeating Procrastination. Although every now and then I might have felt afraid of attempting several tasks simultaneously, I have never, ever, said "no" to myself. When things had not gone well, instead of being afraid, I attempted new approaches, and to benefit from criticisms, even from my enemies. Example # 1 coming my mind was the enormous number of attempts to be the first professor able to become PhD without a mentor. I had to do four pre-defenses instead of one in two different languages, and present seven exams instead of four because I had to go to Ukraine to finish my first PhD going through two universities and three research institutions. I can affirm that, facing opposition, whenever I fell, as soon as possible, I stood up believing in my own possibilities to finish whatever I had started.

- **Tip #5.** Eliminating distractions. I am perseverant and tenacious in whatever undertaking I had been immersed in; therefore, whenever I felt overwhelmed with tasks, I always prioritized the most important ones. As far as I can remember, I have never, ever, left any task unfinished be it working in Cuba, Mexico, the former Soviet Union, and the United States.

- **Tip #6.** Rewarding myself. I have always rewarded myself according to my financial, academic, and scholarly resources. The best reward I have ever obtained is to see the introduction and materialization of working hard. To be recipient of the Excellence in Teaching Award at DePaul University in 2017 – which is annually granted to around ten professors out of close to 900 faculty- was the highest recognition I received during my fifty-four years as faculty in Cuba, Mexico, and United States.

- **Tip #7.** Placing my right hand on my chest, I can affirmed that I had never been a victim of procrastination. I have always been a tenacious person since I was a child under my mother's adorable example. There were two formidable women so far in my eighty-two years of age: my mother, and my second wife.

This author's biggest victories against procrastination were to hold and to conquer a first PhD in Mathematics Applied to Economics, and the second PhD in Economic, Planning, and Organization in the application of economic mathematical models in the Cuban Sugar Industry. As far as I know, I am the third professor holding two PhD in Economics in Cuba. Both degrees were granted in the city of Kiev, Ukraine, in 1982 and 1990.

My biggest political victory was in 1996 when I could escape from the Cuban Communism and became faculty in the United States. I was teaching for fifty -four years approximately to 10,000 students in Cuba, Mexico, and United States.

## Food for thought

1.  This author strongly recommends the readers to think about the seven tips, and to analyze whether they remember to have gone through any of them in the process of making an important decision. Maybe it would be a good idea to reconsider issues or situations in which they might have followed, at least partially, some of the seven tips. If their answers are "yes", were they satisfied with the results of their decisions by going through the tips?

# CHAPTER IV

## Does the pair tenacity and patience play a necessary role in making important decisions?

**"Many of life's failures are people who did not realize how close they were to success when they gave up."**
Thomas A. Edison.

**"There is no passion to be found playing small — in settling for a life that is less than the one you are capable of living."**
Nelson Mandela.

**"Your life's work is to find your life's work and then to exercise the discipline, tenacity, and hard work it takes to pursue it."**
Oprah Winfrey.

**"The most difficult thing is the decision to act. The rest is merely tenacity. The fears are paper tigers. You can do anything you decide to do."**
Amelia Earhart.

**"Life is inherently risky. There is only one big risk you should avoid at all costs, and that is the risk of doing nothing."**
Denis Witley.

**"Through perseverance, many people win success out of what seemed destined to be certain failure."**
Benjamin Disraeli.

**"Patience and tenacity are worth more than twice their weight of cleverness."**
Thomas Huxley

**"A failure is not always a mistake. It may simply be the best one can do under the circumstances. The real mistake is to stop trying."**
B. F. Skinner.

In this author's opinion and personal experience, before letting tenacity display its beneficial effect in the decision-making process, it is convenient to be patient for a time – depending on the complexity, seriousness, and immediateness of the issue to be solved– to make sure that the best available decision has been adequately analyzed.

As far as making good decision on health issues, to be healthy has always been my first priority; therefore, as soon as I observe any sort of abnormality in my body, I rush to make a doctor's appointment.

Since I was a child, my mother was always taking care of my health and took me to the doctor as soon as she could.

The most serious health issues have so far been: 1 - my heart attack in 1998. This was an unforgettable experience in which my wife played a very important role. The post operatory sessions consisted, not only of physical exercises, but also of projection of films related to creating healthy eating, drinking, and sleeping habits, as well as the gradual reduction of weight. I am one of the heart patients of the group I was part of, who immersed himself in the systematic care of his health. It took tenacity not to return to eating fats, fried eggs, to include only fruits in his breakfast for decades, to exercise systematically, as part of physical therapy sessions related to improving my balance, avoiding falls, reducing incontinence, and so on. 2- my triple open-heart operation in 2017 to cure my ascending aortic aneurysm, one blocked artery, and to substitute a valve in my heart. My excellent physical condition made it possible for me to have a successful operation which allowed me to start walking the same day of the operation, to go through a cardiac rehab two days after the operation, to renew exercising, and to go back to normality after three weeks. 3- In 2019 I was prognosed stenosis in my neck and some parts of my vertebral column, which was not recommended to be operated given my, then, seventy-nine years old age. Fortunately, I was not in pain. I was prescribed physical therapy as a way to improve my health. Right away I started a six-week session, whose recommended exercises I have been practicing systematically for two years now.

Since 2017 I have observed systematic improvement of my health due to the following reasons: a) methodical exercising daily during seven consecutive years; b) my balance has increased considerably; c) eating healthily avoiding all types of drinks, saturated fats, fried food, beef, pork, seafood, and salty food; d) I had never smoked and scarcely drank small amounts of alcohol; e) I had a benign tumor in the bladder which was magnifically operated in Greece; f) I systematically take all my medicines, even when I am staying abroad during my frequent trips around the world; g) since mid-August 2022 I have self-assigned the task of walking one mile per day, although in reality, my average is 2.5 miles.

There is a special mention about my health when on September 4th, 2022, in Paris, I paid homage to Victor Hugo walking 7.5 miles during nine hours from the hotel close to the Arch of Triumph to the Pantheon. I walked slowly, enjoying the beauty of the city of Paris, singing, taking photos, enjoying life. As a result of this physical effort, I did not have any pain either in my legs, waist, or hip. On my way back to the hotel I took two trains. It was hard to believe, even for me, that being almost eighty-two years old, I was able to walk almost eight miles feeling very well.

An additional way to make my life more enjoyable is to introduce variety on my exercises, measuring my progress with enthusiasm, exercising an average of two hours per day, sleeping soundly at least seven hours per day. I also enjoying writing manuscripts and publishing my fourteen books with two publishers. In other words, I am always busy following my unforgettable late wife's advice to continue enjoying life after her death.

Remembering retrospectively while I was a young man, always busy studying, working, taking care of my children especially after my divorce with their mother, sometimes I made fast decisions. My tenacity sometimes demanded fast actions, and as a result not always I was successful.

The more complex is the decision to be made, then patience will allow extra time to make up one's mind, and to behave in a tenacious way.

## Food for thought

1.  Some years ago, when visiting one of my best friend's home, a poster caught my attention because it related to "family rules" through the following recommendations, that is to say, "never give up" "keep your promises" "say please and thank you" "be thankful and gracious" "do what you love" "say I love you… then say it again" "you are loved" "try something new" "say I am sorry" "forgive and forget" "make good choices" and "laugh a lot."

2.  Can the readers make a connection between the title of this chapter:" tenacity and patience in relation to making important decisions?" with any of the thirteen phrases of the poster?

3.  Is any of them related to patience, tenacity, and procrastination?

# CHAPTER V
## To Feel or to Getting Older?

**"Those who love deeply never grow old; they may die of old age, but they die young."**
Benjamin Franklin 84

**"To resist the frigidity of old age, one must combine the body, the mind, and the heart. And to keep these in parallel vigor one must exercise, study, and love"**
Karl Von Bonstetten 87 years

**"The excitement of learning separates youth from old age. As long as you're learning you're not old".**
Rosalyn S. Yalow 101 years

**"You can't help getting older, but you don't have to get old".**
George Burns 100 years

**"Let us never know what old age is. Let us know the happiness time brings, not count the years"**
Ausonius 69 years

**"Old age is like climbing a mountain. You climb from ledge to ledge. The higher you get, the more tired and breathless you become, but your views become more extensive"**

Ingmar Bergman 89 years

I have started this special chapter about feeling old with six famous phrases from special people. I have found out their ages, which have been placed to the right of their names. All of them wrote about enjoying old age. Out of the six persons: two lived 100 years, three lived (84 – 89) years, and only one slightly less than 70. This author learned about their ages, after choosing them among sixty famous personalities writing about old age. It falls by itself that they were outstanding representatives of getting older but feeling younger, which is confirmed by reading their activities. Summary of their extraordinary skills:

- Benjamin Franklin was a leading intellectual writer, scientist, printer, inventor, and political philosopher.
- Karl Von Bonstetter was a famous writer in German and French with cosmopolitan interest.
- Rosalyn Yalow, famous American medical physicist, Premio Nobel in medicine.
- George Burns, American comedian, actor, singer, and writer.
- Ausonius, Roman poet tutor of emperor Gratian,
- Ingmar Bergman, Swedish film director, screenwriter, producer and playwright, accomplished filmmaker. Widely considered one of the greatest and most in-fluential filmmakers of all time, his films are known as

"profoundly personal meditations into the myriad struggles facing the psyche and the soul.

It is for this author a big honor to cite these six famous gigantic historical human beings as obvious examples of persons who never felt old.

The author has been inspired to write his own version about this topic as follows:

> "Lucky are human beings who understand old age as a natural process, through which they kept a feeling of being eternally younger useful to humanity."

From Wikipedia.org and www.britannica.com, this author has copied important data about Mr. George Burns.

"Burns remained in good health for most of his life, in part thanks to a daily exercise regimen of swimming, walks, sit-ups, and push-ups. He bought new Cadillacs every year and drove until the age of 93. After that, Burns had chauffeurs drive him around. In his later years, he also had difficulty reading fine print.

Burns suffered a head injury after falling in his bathtub in July 1994 (at 94) and underwent surgery to remove fluid in his skull. Burns never fully recovered and his performing career came to an end. In February 1995 (at 95), Burns, in what would be his final television appearance, was presented with the very first SAG Lifetime Achievement Award by the Screen Actors Guild. In December of that year, a month before his 100th birthday, Burns was well enough to attend a Christmas party hosted by Frank Sinatra (who turned 80 that month), where he reportedly caught the flu, which weakened him further. When Burns was 96, he had signed a lifetime contract with Caesars Palace in Las Vegas to perform stand-up comedy there, which included the guarantee of a show on his centenary, January 20, 1996. When that day came, however, he was too weak to deliver the planned performance. He released a statement joking how he would love for his 100th birthday to have "a night with Sharon Stone."

On March 9, 1996, 49 days after his centenary, Burnes died in his Beverly Hills home.[17] His funeral was held three days later at the Wee Kirk o' the Heather church in Forest Lawn Memorial Park Cemetery, Glendale.[17] As much as he looked forward to reaching the age of 100, Burns also stated, about a year before he died, that he also looked forward to death, saying that on the day he would die, he would be with Gracie again in Heaven. Upon being interred with Gracie, the crypt's marker was changed from, "Grace Allen Burns—Beloved Wife And Mother (1902–1964)" to "Gracie Allen (1902–1964) & George Burns (1896–1996)—Together Again". George had always said that he wanted Gracie to have top billing."

As an important conclusion of the previous notes about Mr. Burns, this author summarizes that to be old is an advantage for the human beings who have been able to successfully exceed seventy or eighty years old. They only had two options: to be old or to die. It would be interesting to add the following questions: how do they feel arriving at those ages? Are they optimist, proud of getting that old, keeping being happy and looking forward with a deep desire to be a healthy and independent person? If the readers' answer is "yes", then, please, place them in the group of optimistic elderly people.

I am in control of my health. After having a heart attack in 1998, and receiving inspirational talks about keeping in good shape, reducing weight, systematic exercising, and optimistic, yes, I was willing and able to fulfill with the main components of a healthy life. Does it mean that I don't take medicines? No, does it mean that it was easy to include physical exercising into an important condition to live longer and healthier? No, it wasn't easy, but I did it. Why could I do it? First of all I had several advantages such as: 1) I had never smoked a single cigarette and much less a cigar {despite the fact that when I was twenty I was an employee of the H.Upmann cigar factory in Havana, who every morning found 5 cigars on his desk}. After I had accumulated more than one hundred cigars, I distributed them free of charge to people walking around the factory; 2) I have never drank alcohol, excluding some exceptional occasions, in which I was morally forced among young men to show my masculinity by drinking a cup of rum. So, after turning 30, 40. 50. 60, 70, 80 (oh my God how many decades!) I had always rejected drinking, not only alcohol, but also coffee or tea. Whenever I was consistently asked how, by being a Cuban, I did not have a cup of coffee, I simply answered. Because I do not need to be alert, to be fully awake, to be active. My nervous system doesn't need any additional drink not to fall asleep or to keep openeyed in my collective participations.

It is not easy to understand how (being a member of a family composed of a father, a mother, one brother, and two sisters who were used to have three or four cups of coffee every day) the youngest person of the family was so energetic that he would not need become extra-energetic by drinking coffee.

Now, there is something special in my personality. I have always been very tenacious. I never said "no" to myself in relation to a task, or an assignment received or created by myself. After receiving a negative response, since I was a youngster, I have always kept trying other ways to materialize my legitimate dreams, wishes, or assignments.

As I was becoming a student, a teacher, a professor, a faculty colleague; and, therefore, being interacting with different persons, I noticed that, spontaneously, without any previous conscious intention, I was different in goals, love for working, and sharing my life with several women. Not to smoke, not to drink was considered to be not socially agreeable for the majority of my friends. By the way. I always loved to read, to study, to do research, to write to constantly learn about diverse topics. This behavior was not very common in Cuba, especially in poor or in middle class neighborhoods.

In this author's eight decades he was always self-assigning hard tasks. He felt the need to succeed, to advance, especially after turning twenty years old.

As a result of this demanding attitude to myself, I was the first member of the family to go to college, to be appointed as a teacher at the University of Havana. My mother was always encouraging me to be tenacious following her example. She learned how to read and write when she was fifty one, and finished high school when she was seventy years old.

This writer had his heart attack when he was 57; by reaching 81 years old, he is full of life because of his attitude to fight against unhealthy methods or procedures. He is a member of the elderly people who would not be afraid of getting old.

This author will attempt to have more "colleagues" in the group of people who don't feel old, but simply get older adding healthy years and optimistic behaviors to their lives.

**Food for thought:**

1. Does increase in seniority necessarily reduce courage to enjoy life?
2. Is procrastination an enemy of living younger and longer with good health?
3. Would tenacity help in defeating procrastination?

# CHAPTER VI
## The incompatible duo tenacity and procrastination

**"I think of myself as something of a connoisseur of procrastination, creative and dogged in my approach to not getting things done."**
Susan Orlean,

**"Tomorrow is the only day in the year that appeals to a lazy man."**
Attributed to Jimmy Lyons

**"Procrastination is the thief of time"**
Charles Dickens

**"You cannot escape the responsibility of tomorrow by evading it today"**
Abraham Lincoln

**"The greatest amount of wasted time is the time not getting started"**
Dawson Trotman

About the book *Solving the Procrastination Puzzle* (A concise guide to strategies for change) by Dr. Timothy A. Pychil

Main points of this book are the following:

1. Definition of procrastination: "Procrastination is the voluntary delay of an intended action despite the knowledge that this delay may harm the individual in terms of the task performance or even just how the individual feels about the task or him or herself. Procrastination is a needless voluntary delay".

2. According to Dictionary.com, Procrastination is the act or habit of procrastinating, or putting off or delaying, especially something requiring immediate attention:

**Traits of procrastination**: 1. <u>Conscientiousness</u> (responsible, scrupulous, persevering, and fussy or tidy. Negatively associated with procrastination, conscientiousness is a resilient factor against unnecessary delay. 2. <u>Emotional instability</u> (neuroticism) nervous, worrisome, or anxious, tense, irritable, pression, shy, impulsiveness and not self-confident. 3.<u>Impulsiveness</u> (act before thinking, low self-control, impulsivity reflects less ability to consider the consequences of one's actions. 4<u>. Self-efficacy</u> to do what is necessary to achieve a desired outcome. It reflects self-confidence and competence. 5. <u>Self-esteem.</u> We perceive ourselves as being relatively close to being the people we want to be. 6. <u>Socially prescribed perfectionist.</u> They believe that others hold unrealistic expectations for their behavior. They believe that others expect them to be perfect, and they feel compelled to try to live up to these expectations.

In summary, the preceding paragraphs deals with a classification of personalities.

**Personality risks:** emotional instability, impulsiveness, socially prescribed perfectionism (traits related to procrastinating individuals).

**Personality resilience:** conscientiousness, self-efficacy, self-esteem procrastination (traits related to non-procrastinating individuals).

**The word tenacity is not mentioned at all in the book.** The closer word to tenacity mentioned in the book is will power, which is the control exerted to do something or restrain impulses.

According to Google, Tenacity is the quality or fact of being able to grip something firmly; grip.

About the book *The End of Procrastination* by Petr Ludwig and Adela Schicker

I was browsing through the index of the book or the summaries at the beginning of the book about eight positive things to be learn in the book; namely, Why people procrastinate? What decision paralysis is, and why it has such a negative effect on us. How human motivation works and how to properly set it in order to work in the long-term? How to find a personal vision, define your strength, and use them to do meaningful things. How your brain works from the perspective of self-control. **How to strengthen your willpower?** How to increase your efficiency. How to learn new positive habits and unlearn the bad ones? How to organize tasks and time so that you can do more without getting tired? How to manage you on failures better and how to overcome the fear of change.

I was looking for the word "tenacity" browsing through the book, and I did not find it. The only question that gave me some sense of the one related to willpower was cognitive resources.

Increasing Your Cognitive Resources. When someone is said to have a strong will, this usually means that the capacity of his or her cognitive resources is very large. The bigger your glass is, the longer you can self-regulate.

In contrast, procrastinators have a very low capacity for self-regulation, and therefore their riders become rapidly exhausted. Current research indicates that willpower can be compared to a muscle. It is possible to strengthen it through training; this will help improve the performance of the riders.

This book doesn't get into how to build or develop willpower; therefore, in this author's opinion the omission of the word tenacity, or iron will as an instrument to defeat procrastination is not clearly exposed in this book.

Which is the difference between willpower and tenacity, according **to** www.bing.com?. **As nouns the difference between willpower and tenacity** is that **willpower** is the unwavering strength of will to carry out one's wishes; while **tenacity** is the quality or state of being tenacious; as, tenacity, or retentiveness, of memory; tenacity, or persistency, of purpose.

In conclusion, which are the synonyms of procrastination and tenacity?

**What is the synonym of procrastination?** Procrastination: a state, a habit, or an instance of being slow or late about doing something that should be done. Synonyms: avoidance, delay, waiting… Antonyms: alacrity, eagerness, readiness…

**What is a synonym for tenacity?** Some common synonyms of tenacity are courage, mettle, resolution, and spirit. While all these words mean "mental or moral strength to resist opposition, danger, or hardship," tenacity adds to resolution implications of stubbornness, persistence, and unwillingness to admit defeat, holding to their beliefs with great determination.

*This author came across an interesting paper related to defeating procrastination which is resumed as follows:*

## 5 Mind Tricks That Can Help You Defeat Procrastination by Mr. Jack Krier, American writer

> "Procrastination is driven by a variety of thoughts and habits, but fundamentally, we avoid tasks or put them off because we do not believe we'll enjoy doing them and want to avoid making ourselves unhappy, or we fear that we won't do them well."

As such, instead of facing potentially unpleasant work, our mind turns to more enjoyable ideas. That's where a controlled mindset comes to fruition.

By changing our thought patterns when it comes to work and distractions, we stop the causes of procrastination before they take over our days. On this basis, here are five mind tricks that can help you defeat procrastination.

## Trick #1: Get to know the master procrastinator in your mind

Many people see themselves as "habitual procrastinators." *I never get anything done. I start my days well, but when the first distractions appear, my productivity is gone.* Some people struggle more with procrastination than others, but we all have a human tendency to avoid uncomfortable situations. In other words, we all have a master procrastinator in our minds.

## Trick #2: Ask your future self for advice

Another mind trick to avoid procrastination is to consult your future self. Next time you realize that your focus is slipping — and that some kind of distraction is taking your mind off work, pause for five minutes and ask a simple question: "What would my future self say about this?" The trick will help you understand the effects of your procrastination.

## Trick #3: Combine instant gratification with habits that include long-term rewards

Much like asking your future self for advice, speeding up the long-term advantages of uncomfortable activities is a powerful anti-procrastination tool.

## Trick #4: Separate essential and non-essential things in your mind

Many people procrastinate as a result of multitasking. In this context, we have a million to-dos and fail to distinguish between the ones we need to complete today and the ones that can wait. That's where the separation of "essential" and "non-essential" tasks comes into play.

## Trick #5: Get your mind into the best possible starting position

Finally, to defeat procrastination once and for all, you need to get your mind into the right starting position. In short, eliminate all the thoughts, ideas, and mindsets that could hamper your tenacity.

But what about procrastination as an enemy to live younger and longer with good health?

Tenacity can help overcoming obstacles, which would tend to introduce happiness and success into their lives.

This author will introduce three questions to the readers in order to elicit responses from them. Here they go:

1. Does defeating procrastination open the door to improving tenacity?
2. Does increase in seniority necessarily reduce courage to enjoy life?
3. Would the readers, after reading and studying this book, be able to be tenacious and successful in whatever undertaking they pursue?

Going question by question

## 1. Does defeating procrastination open the door to improving tenacity?

If the reader considers him or herself to be a tenacious person, it falls over by itself that– even in the case of being gritty – the person would most likely have had to feel discouraged, unable, unprepared to battle against procrastination. Life is not a free riding adventure.

This author wants to send a concrete message to the readers of this book: 1. Trust in yourselves. 2. Believe in your possibilities of success against any oppositions which you might find in your way. 3. Be tenacious all the time. Stand up after a fall. 4. Be also prepared to study, to learn, to persevere relentlessly in pursuing your goal. 5. Expect opposition, even from people who you were considering among your friends. 6. Try hard and be sure of the cause that you are dedicating your life to.

Giving an answer to the question which started this part of the book. This author's answer is empathic and decisive "YES" tenacity allows a person to defeat procrastination. In a way, being procrastinating is having doubts about your talents. Be brave and try hard maybe once, twice, thrice, but at the end YOU WILL SUCCEED by defeating procrastination through tenacity.

If the readers go through medical circumstances, and they can understand the reasons for being unhealthy, make up your mind to defend your health for your own benefit and that of your family. They will be proud of you because they can see that you are battling, not only for your personal health, but also for theirs. Your family needs you, and you need your family. Think about how happy they will be when they feel that you are strictly following your doctors' instructions to keep you, not only alive, but also healthy. You are paving the way towards a healthy old age. Not being afraid of all age, but rather being thankful to God for optimistically arriving at an old age.

## 2. Does increase in seniority necessarily reduce courage to enjoy life?

Definitely no. If a senior loved to enjoy life when he/she was young, then this person will continue feeling almost the same when he/she gets old. For a person to be happy during old age, he/she most likely would have been happy during their youths.

Citing the case of the author's mother and father. His two parents were hard workers through all their lives. His mother was always looking for something else to do. So, she could fulfill all her home chores and had also time for helping other people in social activities, sowing clothes for children, and so on. She enjoyed being useful to humanity. When she died at 88 she had not lost courage to enjoy life. At her last Christmas festivity, maybe she wasn't careful enough in drinking wine, and started to feel sick. She was sent to the hospital, where she died in peace one week later.

His father, during his youth, was a hard worker, never missing one workday, without any vacations. He was extremely healthy but was not a happy man because his infidelities at old age were not accepted by his wife. He still was in love with her, but she couldn't stay close to him. They were sleeping in different bedrooms. In other words, she didn't lose courage to enjoy life, in her old age, but without him. He couldn't be happy without her.

In conclusion the author's mother was full of courage to enjoy life in her senior years, while his father did not experience courage to be happy without her love. Seniority did not directly contribute to reduce courage to enjoy life in this senior couple.

Going to church every week, I met seniors in an advanced age beyond 90, who did not appear to be enjoying life. They were kind and helpful to all the parishioners, but their faces did not show happiness or enthusiasm. There was an exception of one hundred years old priest, who was always having a smile in his face even during the uncertain years of the pandemic. He never lost courage to enjoy life.

On the other extreme, there was a middle-aged man, with a magnificent tenor voice, whose face was generally contracted, or sad either to shorten or to undergo an increase in tension. He never spoke about his girlfriend, wife, or close feminine companion. Suddenly one day, some parishioner brought the sad news that our tenor had died of unknown reason.

The eldest parishioner of our church was 105 years old. He was always optimist, encouraging people to participate in the coffee-hour activity, and to keep an optimistic and friendly face. He travelled extensively by cruises even though he had difficulty in walking. He enjoyed life by visiting foreign countries although he had never been accompanied. Nobody knew any lovely relation of this man, but he was always ready to be friendly and to share his experiences as a traveler of the world.

This author was married to two ladies: one of them made him father on two occasions, but he was not happy with her because of their different sexual drives. After unfortunate 10-year coexistence they got divorced, but he was always a good father and was able to enjoy fatherhood at its best observing how his two children followed his same way as students and good citizens.

Both children always obeyed rules and laws, helping others, protecting old age, telling an adult if someone is a danger to themselves or others, being responsible for their own actions, and finally being exemplary students and loving their both parents.

The author's second wife was one of a kind lady. She could not become a mother because on five occasions she lost her fetuses. Nonetheless, her marriage was the best gift that he could receive from God. She was so extraordinary that she trained him not to suffer after death. He wrote a book paying homage to her exceptional human nature. Seven years after her death in his arms, he is still in love with her. His reiterated joy comes from having become an empathetic man during their last year together. They spent 40 years, 6 months and one day in love with each other.

From this author's knowledge of mathematics, and mathematical statistics, he learned that it is very difficult to prove that some characteristic of phenomenon is always true. But with a few examples, the opposite can be proven right.

The question at the title of this part of the book, namely does increase in seniority reduce courage to enjoy life was proven false because in the six examples, only in the case of his mother, one of two priests, his wife and himself have shown the following results: if an individual is happy while being young and have the courage to enjoy life, chances are that he will continue enjoying life in his old age. But if an individual is generally very reserved to himself, does not show joy as a habit, most likely he will not show courage to enjoy life if he reaches an old age.

This author can affirm about himself that — although he had been very busy studying and learning in a systematic way — he also had time to sing, to dance, and to feel the courage to enjoy life while he was getting ready to complete his two doctorates. His wife, Gladys, also contributed considerably to make a happy man of him, by making him empathetic. After her death he started a prolific career as a writer, inspirational speaker, and singer paying homage to her. He is also very busy becoming a househusband. He keeps very busy also travelling around the world. Therefore, he can illustrate the example of a person who can stand up after a fall, and be busy enjoying life. No time for thinking about being lonely. She is alive in his memory . In conclusion he is an example of an old man whose seniority is very active and happy. He is not afraid of getting old. Going further, he is not afraid to die because he is creating a legacy teaching through his books. Consequently, when the time comes for him to die, he will continue living through his books.

Finally, some advice to all seniors approaching late seventies or early eighties to keep dreaming about being healthy, useful to society and to themselves, and very especially to keep busy. It is wonderful to ask oneself, what shall I do now. I am full of things and tasks to do.

In conclusion through the different examples, this author couldn't prove that, generally speaking, an increase in seniority reduces courage to enjoy life. Physical exercise is an excellent way to keep healthy and happy.

## Tenacity and the need of suffering inherent to being tenacious

My son just sent me an electronic paper, which has caught my attention to the point that I am adding its main content to this chapter.

The title of the paper is : "Why a meaningful life is impossible without suffering – Big Think". It can be consulted at "HTTPS://BIGTHINK.COM/the-well/paul-bloom-meaning-suffering"

I am copying three phrases, which have caught my attention, and made me meditate:

1.  "From an evolutionary perspective, it makes sense that we feel pain: It trains us to avoid experiences, or stimuli that harm us"

2. "But that begs the question, why do so many people choose to pursue things that will bring them pain?

3. Top psychologist Paul Bloom's answer is that living a meaningful life requires that we choose to take on a reasonable amount of pain"

Through most of my life I have been tenacious in overcoming huge obstacles, but so far, I have never thought about feeling pain while I was in the process of achieving successes.

While I am sure not to have suffered physical pain in the process of holding the first or the second PhD, I had to fight with psychological pain.

From the previously cited paper, I am taking two interesting paragraphs with which I am totally in agreement because I do know what it means to feel psychological pain in the process of achieving successful scholarly results.

"Intense 'unbearable' mental (psychological) pain is defined as an emotionally based extremely aversive feeling which can be experienced as torment. It can be associated with a psychiatric disorder or with a severe emotional trauma such as the death of a child."

Psychogenic pain is not an official diagnostic term. It is used to describe a pain disorder attributed to psychological factors. Such things as beliefs, fears, and strong emotions can cause, increase, or prolong pain"

"What is the difference between physical and mental pain?

Pain has two components: a sensory component (physical) and an emotional or affective component (psychological). The former informs your body where the pain is coming from, while the latter causes psychological distress after an experience of pain.

People often think of pain as a purely physical sensation. However, pain has biological, psychological, and emotional factors. Furthermore, chronic pain can cause feelings such as anger, hopelessness, sadness, and anxiety. Yet, short of catastrophic injuries or illnesses, emotional pain often impacts our lives far more than physical pain does"

From psychology today.com, this author found an interesting paper written by Guy Winch PhD, which is summarized as follows:

**"5 ways Emotional Pain is worse than physical pain"**

**"Why emotional pain causes longer-lasting damage to our lives?**

We tend to monitor our bodies and our physical health far more than we do our emotional health. For example, we get yearly physical check-ups but the idea of getting a 'psychological check-up' is completely foreign to us.

We know that if a small physical injury like a cut becomes more painful over time it is a sign of a more serious infection. But if failing to get a promotion at work is still emotionally painful after several weeks we are unaware that we might be getting depressed.

We tend to react to physical pain much more proactively than we do to emotional pain. Yet, short of catastrophic injuries or illnesses, emotional pain often impacts our lives far more than physical pain does. Here are five reasons emotional pain is worse than physical pain:

1. Memories Trigger Emotional Pain But Not Physical Pain: Recalling the time you broke your leg will not make your leg hurt but recalling the time you felt rejected by your high-school crush will cause you substantial emotional pain. Our ability to evoke emotional pain by merely remembering distressing events is profound and stands in stark contrast to our total inability (thankfully) to re-experience physical pain.

2. We Use Physical Pain as Distraction from Emotional Pain Not Vice Versa: Some teens and adults practice 'cutting' (slicing their flesh superficially with a blade) because the physical pain it evokes distracts them from their emotional pain, thus offering them relief. But the same does not work in reverse, which is why we rarely see a woman choosing to manage the pain of natural childbirth by re-reading the rejection letter from her college of choice. Unfortunately, although we might prefer physical to emotional pain, others see our pain differently.

3. Physical Pain Garners Far More Empathy from Others Than Emotional Pain: When we see a stranger get hit by a car we wince, gasp, or even scream and run to see if they're OK. But when we see a stranger get bullied or taunted, we are unlikely to do any of those things. Studies found we consistently underestimate others' emotional pain but not their physical pain. Further, these empathy gaps for emotional pain are reduced only if we've experienced a similar emotional pain very recently ourselves.

4. Emotional Pain Echoes in Ways Physical Pain Does Not: If you got a call about your parent dying while you

were having a romantic lobster meal with your partner on Valentine's Day, it will probably be a few years before you can enjoy lobster or Valentine's Day without becoming extremely sad. But if you broke your foot playing softball in an amateur league you will likely be back on the field as soon as you're fully healed. Physical pain usually leaves few echoes (unless the circumstance of the injury was emotionally traumatic) while emotional pain leaves numerous reminders, associations, and triggers that reactivate our pain when we encounter them.

5.  Emotional Pain but Not Physical Pain Can Damage Our Self-Esteem and Long-Term Mental Health: Physical pain has to be quite extreme to affect our personalities and damage our mental health (again, unless the circumstances are emotionally traumatic as well) but even single episodes of emotional pain can damage our emotional health. For example, failing an exam in college can create anxiety and a fear of failure, a single painful rejection can lead to years of avoidance and loneliness, bullying in middle school can make us shy and introverted as adults, and a critical boss can damage our self-esteem for years to come.

For all these are reasons we should give our emotional health just as much (if not more) attention and care as we do our physical health. Alas, we rarely do. While we take action at the first sight of a sniffle or muscle sprain, we do little to 'treat' common emotional injuries such as rejection, failure, guilt, brooding, or loneliness when we sustain them. While we apply antibacterial ointment to a cut or scrape right away, we do little to boost or protect our self-esteem when it is low.

True, we might not know what actions we can take in such situations, but the good news is that this kind of information is readily available. All we must do is seek it out (for example, by using the search function on this website).

https://www.psychologytoday.com/gb/blog/the."

I am citing the five reasons why emotional pain is worse than physical pain:

1) Memories Trigger Emotional Pain But Not Physical Pain.
2) We Use Physical Pain as Distraction from Emotional Pain Not Vice Versa
3) Physical Pain Garners Far More Empathy from Others Than Emotional Pain:
4) Emotional Pain Echoes in Ways Physical Pain Does Not:
5) Emotional Pain but Not Physical Pain Can Damage Our Self-Esteem and Long-Term Mental Health."

As a conclusion summarizing the five reasons I can relate them to the main enemy of tenacity, namely procrastination.

Why? If anybody is physically sick, it is, generally speaking, not a shame to let other people know that he/she needed help in searching for a medicine or a doctor's appointment.

But, if -on the contrary anybody needs help fighting against procrastination- (such as presenting a scholarly paper in public, or even a dissertation to a group of colleagues) this individual is victim of his own self-esteem.

The procrastination grows roots in human being's brains. I am very lucky to have always fought against procrastination, even though not always I had been aware of its influence and power.

**Food for thought**

**After reading and meditating about the contents of this book, can the readers?**

1. identify the circumstances that can make them a prey of procrastination?
2. be more psychologically prepared to overcome procrastination?
3. be more prepared to become tenacious and successful in whatever undertaking they pursue?